From the Pacific to the Atlantic CANADA'S GIGANTIC!

NADA'S

GIGANT

From the Pacific to the Atlantic CANADA'S GIGANTIC!

Photographs by Henri Robideau / Text by Peter Day
Summerhill Press, Toronto

© **1988 Henri Robideau and Peter Day**

Canadian Cataloguing in Publication Data
Robideau, Henri, 1946–
    From the Pacific to the Atalantic — Canada's gigantic

ISBN 0-920197-45-0

1. Canada — Description and travel — 1981–
Views. 2. Canada — Description and travel —
1981 —   — Miscellanea.   I. Title.   II. Title:
Canada's gigantic.

FC75.R62 1988   971.064'7'0222   C88-093618-5
F1017.R62 1988

Typesetting: Type a Grafik, Toronto
Design: Lisa Naftolin
Printed and bound in Canada
Distributed in Canada by
The University of Toronto Press
5201 Dufferin Street
Downsview, Ontario, M3H 5T8

For Jeannie

Introduction

Henri Robideau is a photographer with works in the collections of the Vancouver and Winnipeg art galleries, the Canadian Centre for Contemporary Photography in Ottawa, the Photographers Gallery in Saskatoon and the Canada Council Art Bank. He is also a Gianthropologist.

Robideau has travelled from the Pacific to the Atlantic on "digs" in search of gigantic things, oversized monuments like the giant Canada Goose in Wawa, Ontario; the giant Mountie on horseback in North Battleford, Saskatchewan; Christ overlooking a valley of dinosaurs in Drumheller, Alberta; the giant 12-sided nickel in Sudbury, Ontario; the giant metal Ukrainian Easter Egg in Vegreville, Alberta; and the giant Sasquatch in Williams Lake, British Columbia. In the last fifteen years Robideau has photographed over one hundred and fifty Giant Things across Canada.

While some Giant Things are monuments, others are functional buildings. He has found a church in Inuvik, Northwest Territories, built in the shape of an igloo; a bungalow in Thunder Bay, Ontario, with an addition in the form of giant Dutch wooden shoe; a giant lobster trap restaurant and souvenir shop in Cheticamp, Nova Scotia; and, in St. Jean, Quebec, a drive-in restaurant in the form of an orange. In the centre of Leamington, Ontario, (which describes itself as the "Tomato Capital of Canada") Robideau came across a giant red tomato tourist information booth. In 1984, while on a "dig" in northern Ontario, Robideau found the Midas Chipmobile, a giant muffler-shaped mobile chip stand, in Sudbury. On the same dig, near Beardmore, he uncovered a giant snowman ice cream vending stand.

Robideau gathers his material in rather random and unscientific ways. "Somebody tells me about where this or that giant thing is, or else I find it myself just by cruising around and bumping into it." The Giant Things he has found and photographed on his digs form an endearing, if somewhat amusing, portrait of Canada. It is no surprise really that Merike Talve has dubbed him a "surrealist archivist". "I call a dig a dig because not only do I really dig those like far-out-man giant things, but because that's what Gianthropologists *do*. They go out on digs."

Robideau was born in 1946 in Bristol, Connecticut, into a Franco-American family with roots in Quebec. After spending his teenage years in California, he moved to Vancouver in 1970 and found work as a photographic technician in the historical photograph section of the Vancouver Public Library. There, he began work on a still-unpublished book on Mattie Gunterman, a cook and photographer in the turn-of-the-century Lardeau Gold Rush. He also started documenting the Giant Things he discovered in and around Vancouver.

The first was early in 1973: a giant loaf of bread held aloft by a hand on top of McGavin's Bakery. "It was damaged in a wind storm. I knew that one day it would be pulled down, so I photographed it before it was too late," says Robideau. He was right. The loaf and the hand are no longer there. "I'm glad I got many of them before they went. People don't seem to have the greatest respect for Giant Things and while they may like them today, people are a fickle lot. Tomorrow they'll think the Giant Things are just eyesores and should be torn down." He still regrets missing a giant tea cup that produced real steam that used to be near the Vancouver CN railway station.

In the mid and late 1970s Robideau went on digs up and down the West Coast. Finally, in 1981, with the help of a Canada Council grant, he went further afield, eventually travelling from the Pacific to the Atlantic in search of Giant Things to photograph. In Bonshaw, Prince Edward Island, he found a 2.4 metre long killer ant and in Boissevain, Manitoba, the home of the Turtle

Hall of Fame and the Canadian Turtle Derby, he discovered a 9 metre high turtle standing on its hind legs and waving the Canada flag with one paw and the Manitoba provincial flag with the other.

Giant Things, and the fascination with them, have been found throughout history. Three (some say four) of the Seven Wonders of the Ancient World were Giant Things. One was the Colossus of Rhodes, a giant bronze figure of the sun god Helios, which stood at the entrance to the port on the Mediterrean island of Rhodes. Said to be 30 metres high, this Giant Thing took twelve years to build and was toppled by an earthquake in 224 B.C., barely a half-century after completion.

Giant Things traditionally induced awe and wonder. Phidias's giant gold and ivory statue of Athena dominated the ancient Greek city of Athens and the giant image of the Greek god Jupiter stood at a temple at Olympus. Pliny reports that the Roman emperor Nero had a 32 metre tall statue of himself designed by Zenodorus. Japan still boasts a number of giant statues of the Buddha. The one in the ancient capital of Nara is 16 metres tall and dates from the 8th century A.D. Another in Kamakura is 11.4 metres high.

The list goes on. Michelangelo's giant sculpture of David became a symbol of Florence and Florentine independence. In the 18th and 19th centuries travellers came from all over North America and Europe to see, experience and record giant natural wonders like Niagara Falls, the Grand Canyon and Mount Everest. The Statue of Liberty, a Giant Thing measuring 93 metres high, has become a symbol of the United States and the freedom that country offered to generations of immigrants. And, as with many famous Giant Things the Statue of Liberty is reproduced in a variety of forms as souvenir: Snow shakers, pencil sharpeners, paperweights and keychains and on all manner of t-shirts, postcards and tea towels.

In the 20th century, American Pop artist Claes Oldenburg has proposed, and sometimes installed in cities around the world Giant Things based on mundane consumer products: A giant baseball bat in Chicago, three giant straw hats in a city park in Salinas, California and a giant ice-pick in Kassel, West Germany. Together with architect Frank Gehry, Oldenburg is planning to use a giant pair of binoculars as the entry portals to a Venice, California, office building. California is particularly rich in Giant Things, especially buildings, many dating from the 1920s and 1930s. These modern Giant Things differ from their ancient counterparts in one significant way: They often have a sense of humour.

Robideau has a theory that in the United States most giant things are erected for commercial purposes. They are exotic and incongruous, gimmicks aimed at attracting customers. An example of this is Lucy, James F. Lafferty's

20 metre high elephant, erected in South Atlantic City in 1881 and used as an office for selling real estate. Like Lucy many Giant Things are buildings, but most of these come in the form of the product being sold: A giant ice-cream cone is a summer-time vending stand for ice-cream; a collection of Indian teepees are motel rooms; a giant lobster trap is a fish restaurant. These are three-dimensional bill boards, often placed along the side of a highway, with the intention of catching the eye of motorists. "WOW! Look at that giant hot dog! Let's eat there!" is the desired reaction and the speeding motorist becomes a patron of the hot dog stand.

Though Canada does have its share of giant things that advertise restaurants or shops, Robideau feels that the Canadian motives for erecting a Giant Thing often differ from the Americans' commercial ambitions. In Canada most Giant Things here are put up for reasons of civic pride. Some make a visual play on the town's name. "Like the giant turtle in Turtleford or the moose in Moose Jaw," says Robideau, adding, "though I've often wondered what they'd put up in Dildo, Newfoundland!" Others, like the giant bow and arrow outside Moosomin, Saskatchewan, or the giant golf ball near Sorel, Quebec, are roadsigns indicating an entrance or turn-off – in these cases to an archery range and to a golf club respectively.

Many are memorials, erected on an anniversary, to mark a notable event in the town's history. The larger-than-life-size concrete sculpture of an elephant in the southwestern Ontario town of St. Thomas was created by Winston Bronnum of Sussex, New Brunswick to commemorate the centenary of the death in 1885 of Jumbo the circus elephant in that city.

Jumbo's story merits some attention. Then, as now, St. Thomas was split in two by a railway line. P.T. Barnum's circus was in town. It was nine-thirty at night. Barnum's celebrated troupe of thirty-one elephants had done their turn in the ring and was being led back along a section of track to their box cars. At the back of the line was Jumbo, a giant African elephant, followed by Tom Thumb, a young elephant who specialized in stunts. On one side of the track were the box cars and on the other a steep embankment. Suddenly out of the night came the lights and blare of a freight train, an unscheduled special, Number 151 Grand Trunk Railway locomotive. It rammed into Tom Thumb, throwing him down the embankment, then plowed into Jumbo. The impact derailed the locomotive and Jumbo was pinned beneath it. Tom Thumb survived, his leg badly broken but Jumbo was mortally injured and died within hours of the accident. Ever the showman, Barnum concocted his own version of the accident. He put the word out that Jumbo had seen what was about to happen and deliberately stepped in front of the train, thereby sacrificing his life to save the life of little Tom Thumb.

Jumbo, a star attraction during his lifetime, continued to draw the crowds even in death. His body was skinned, stuffed and for two years toured as a side show of the circus. His bones were given to to New York's Museum of Natural History where they are still on view.

A century later a controversy over the placement of Jumbo's memorial divided St. Thomas. Winston Bronnum's giant concrete sculpture of Jumbo was placed on a small square beside the local museum, on a ridge overlooking Highway 3 and the entrance to the town. Visitors entering St. Thomas were greeted with a rear-end view of the elephant! Some townsfolk said this was insulting; others felt that this was appropriate, because after all, Jumbo had been "rear-ended" by the locomotive.

Giant Things like Jumbo are landmarks on the map of Canada. You know you've arrived in Rocanville, Saskatchewan, when as you drive along Highway 8 you see the 6.5 metre high oil can on the outskirts of town. It was in Rocanville in 1923 that Ernest Symons of Symons Metalworkers, invented the trigger-operated squirting oil can. The Symons Oiler, as it is called, gives a measured squirt of oil through its long, narrow spout – a boon to mechanics and farmers worldwide who had previously contended with an uncontrolled and unmeasured gush from their oil cans. Fifty years later, the town honoured Ernie Symons' invention by installing this memorial, a giant version of the oiler that brought renown to Rocanville – now this landmark helps distinguish Rocanville from other prairie towns.

Robideau expanded on the use of Giant Things as landmarks in a 1984 letter to the editor of the Vancouver *Sun* that explained how he always knew when he was home in Vancouver: "I'll never forget coming in from Kamloops one time, whamming down the Trans Canada through Burnaby, swooping onto the Grandview Highway off-ramp, cruising up across the lights at Boundary Road and dipping down the hill to Renfrew where the Giant Jar of Martini Olives, slowly turning on its base, bid me a friendly 'Hello pal, welcome back to Vancouver – you're home!'"

The letter was prompted by the destruction of this particular Giant Thing. Added Robideau: "I think I can speak for all the Gianthropologists out there when I say 'Goodbye Giant Jar of Olives, rest in peace, we'll miss you.'"

Peter Day

British Columbia

Fearing an attack from the Japanese Navy during the Second World War Vancouver imposed nighttime blackouts and that included even neon lights. Faced with a loss of business, Neon Products, a Vancouver sign company, came up with the idea of erecting giant three-dimensional billboards instead. The company continued erecting them after the war – *Hand and Loaf* was installed in 1947. Alf Farmer, who worked for Neon Products, modelled the hand of this Giant Thing after his own left hand. The loaf was made out of sheet metal and was the size of a summer cottage, claims Robideau. "A friend of mine said that he'd have loved to have lived in there!"

Hand and Loaf, Vancouver, B.C. 1973

British Columbia

Vancouver used to be known for its neon, but in the sixties and seventies it started to go out of fashion. People thought neon signs were tacky, so they took many of them down and replaced them with back-lit plexiglass ones. Happily this giant, neon-trimmed steaming chop suey bowl with chopsticks survived. It serves as the logo for the Ho Ho Chop Suey Restaurant on Pender Street in downtown Vancouver.

Chop Suey Bowl　　　Vancouver, British Columbia　　　1986

British Columbia

This Giant Thing (more correctly a collection of Giant Things) was claimed at the time as the tallest flagpole, the biggest Canadian flag, the largest hockey stick and mightiest puck in the world. They were located on the main Expo 86 site and formed a prominent landmark, and meeting point, at the fair. That was what Norman Hay and John Gallop hoped would happen. Hay was Creative Director of the Canada Pavilion at Expo 86 and John Gallop a designer working with him. They had a problem to solve and both men claim that they each woke up one morning with the idea. The problem was this: The Canada Pavilion was located in Canada Place on Burrard Inlet, a five minute train ride away from the main Expo site on False Creek. The Canada Pavilion needed something special to attract visitors on the Expo site into taking the skytrain to the Canada Pavilion. These symbols of Canada (a giant laminated wood hockey stick, puck, flag pole and Canadian flag) did just that. They were designed by Ed Berwick of the Vancouver architectural firm of Berwick, Thomson and Pratt.

After Expo 86 closed these Giant Things were given to the people of Canada by the Federal Government and have been relocated in Cowichan Bay, Vancouver Island, a small town on the Trans Canada Highway between Duncan and Victoria.

Hockey Stick & Puck, Vancouver, B.C.   1986

British Columbia

Made of sheet metal and realistically painted, this giant jar of martini olives was located on top of a building at the corner of Grandview Highway and Renfrew Street in Vancouver. "When I first moved to Vancouver in 1970, the jar use to revolve, but by the mid seventies, it stopped rotating," says Robideau. "Perhaps the mechanism broke, or the business it was advertising had moved some place else." In 1984, when Robideau took his photograph, the building was being used by a different company, one that sold refrigerators. The jar of olives was no longer appropriate, so eventually it was taken down. "But that company also moved, or went out of business, and they tore down the building and replaced it with a mini-mall."

Olive Jar, Vancouver, B.C. 1984

British Columbia

This 9 metre high concrete statue of the Hindu god Chaitanga Mahaprabru stands in front of a temple belonging to the Krishna Consciousness Society on Southeast Marine Drive in suburban Burnaby. Bright pigments were used in the final cement coating of the figure – the skin is gold and the robe is saffron coloured with a light blue sash. This Giant Thing was sculpted by Subrata Lahiri, a 52 year old graduate of the University of Calcutta, and unveiled on August 18, 1985.

Chaitanya Mahaprabu, Burnaby, B.C.   *1985*

British Columbia

"The Piggy Bank a good example of something that I've run into all the time," says Robideau. "There will be a sign that says the 'world's largest...' or the 'world's only something or other.' How do people know that it really is the largest? Do they go out and do research?" Obviously not, because Robideau had found an even larger Piggy Bank, the size of a railway engine, in Coleman, Alberta. It too claims to be the "Biggest Piggy Bank in the World."

Piggy Bank   *Williams Lake, British Columbia*   *1984*

British Columbia

The Sasquatch (Salish Indian for "wild man" or "hairy man") is a giant, apelike creature that supposedly roams the remoter regions of the West Coast. Mentioned in Indian myth and legends and in the journals of early European travellers in the region, there have even been sightings of Sasquatches in modern times.

This Sasquatch was designed by Paul Sissons and placed in front of his taxidermy shop on Highway 97 outside Williams Lake, British Columbia. The body is made of fibreglass and is covered by brown plush living-room carpet.

Sasquatch   Williams Lake, British Columbia   1981

British Columbia

Mr. PG, short for Mr. Prince George, stands in front of the visitor information centre just outside the city, and acts as a giant three-dimensional billboard, attracting passing motorists. He is the mascot of Prince George (population 67,559), a city that sits at the junction of the Fraser and Nechako Rivers and Highways 16 and 97. Founded in 1807 Prince George was originally named Fort George, after George III, then King of England. It was renamed Prince George in 1915.

The original Mr. PG was made out of spruce wood but was replaced in 1983 by a fibreglass and sheet metal version painted to look like wood. On his head is a yellow hard hat and in his right hand a painted aluminum Canadian flag. A time capsule of articles donated by the Chamber of Commerce, the local art gallery and the media, and representing Prince George in 1983, has been place inside Mr. PG's chest – "Right above his heart," says Bill Jones, Special Projects Officer of Prince George.

Spruce Person   Prince George, British Columbia   1984

British Columbia

Situated on the Columbia River, Revelstoke lies on the Trans Canada Highway, midway between Kamloops, B.C., and Calgary, Alberta. First settled in the mid 1800s, Revelstoke is a forestry, mining and railway town and is named after Lord Revelstoke, whose British bank invested in the Canadian Pacific Railway that runs just west of the town.

Some 9 metres tall, this Giant Thing stands outside the Smokey the Bear Campground, not far from the town. On the buckle of the bear's belt is his name, *Smokey*.

Smokey The Bear   Revelstoke, British Columbia   1982

British Columbia

This giant wooden head was carved in the 1920s out of the base of a tree that originally stood beside the Big Bend Highway, which ran between Revelstoke and Golden
along the Columbia River. Alongside stood a sign that read: "Don't be wooden headed
drive carefully you'll live to enjoy the scenery more and longer."

As result of the Columbia River Treaty, signed in 1961 between Canada and the
United States, three dams were constructed on the Columbia River. These flooded
large parts of the area and to save it from being drowned the head was cut from its
roots, repainted and relocated near downtown Revelstoke.

Wooden Head   Revelstoke, British Columbia   1983

Northwest Territories

This Catholic church is one of a number of churches in the Northwest Territories that are built and painted white, to resemble traditional Inuit igloos. Another such igloo-shaped church is in Baker Lake and another in Frobisher Bay.

Igloo Church   Inuvik, Northwest Territories   1981

Yukon Territory

Whitehorse (population 14,800) has, since 1953, been the capital of the Yukon Territory. "This building is always shown in the guide books as a point of interest in Whitehorse," says Robideau. "It is on a side street, among suburban houses and single-storey log cabins, but this three-storey one is different from its neighbours."

Highrise Log Cabin   Whitehorse, Yukon Territory   1981

Alberta

This Big Thing stands outside of Blairmore, Alberta, beside Highway 3, where it heads west toward the Crow's Nest Pass. At an elevation of 1357 metres above sea level, this pass through the Rocky Mountains is on the border between British Columbia and Alberta. It was this point that the Canadian Pacific Railway selected in 1897 to extend its line to compete with the incursion of American railroads into southwestern Canada.

Crow's nest, Blairmore, Alberta   1984

Alberta

Similar teepee-shaped buildings are common in the United States, especially in the Southwest where they are generally made of stucco. These teepees in Blairmore are made of tar-paper, each is differently coloured, and they serve as motel rooms. The motel office is a giant Conestoga wagon.

Sleepy Teepy Motel   Blairmore, Alberta   1984

Alberta

Jesus and the dinosaurs, Drumheller, Alber

1982

Alberta

≺ Drumheller, located in southern Alberta, 136 kilometres northeast of Calgary lies in the middle of the Badlands, an area rich in dinosaur bones. "There is this place called Prehistoric Park," recalls Robideau. "You pay your entry fee and walk around looking at these concrete dinosaurs, scattered all over the hills. You walk up through this valley, up this hill and at the top there is this dinosaur. Then you turn around and on the hill opposite you there is this 9.1 metre high Jesus with his arms outstretched." He adds: "It appears like a miracle."

These giant dinosaurs and Jesus (called "Christ of the Badland") were built by Tigg Seland. He also made the *Tyrannosaurus rex* in downtown Drumheller and the giant geese in Hanna, Alberta.

Located on Highway 22, southwest of Calgary, Black Diamond has a population of 1,450. Black Diamond is an oil town and this three-dimensional black diamond is a symbol of the wealth that oil bought to the area.

Black Diamond   Black Diamond, Alberta   1984

Alberta

Vegreville (population 5,251) lies 80 kilometres east of Edmonton on Highway 16, popularly called the Yellow Head Highway. This giant *Pysanka*, the proper name for a painted Ukrainian Easter Egg, was designed by Professor Ronald Resch, a computer scientist at the University of Utah. The egg is 7.8 metres long, 9.45 metres tall, 5.5 metres wide and weighs 2,250 kilograms. It is constructed of 3,512 triangular- and star-shaped facets made of aluminum and rotates in the wind.

Dedicated in 1976, this giant egg was erected to mark the centennial in 1974 of presence of the Royal Canadian Mounted Police in Alberta.

Pysanka~ Ukranian Easter Egg , Vegreville, Alberta, 1983

Alberta

Not far from Red Deer is Eckville, a farming community of 842. This giant manure shovel, just outside of town, serves as a three-dimensional logo advertising Marvin and Wilma Wine's family business, Mar-Wil Acres.

Manure Shovel   Eckville, Alberta   1983

Saskatchewan

Snapping turtles (*Chelydra serpentina*), weighing up to 18 kg and measuring 40cm long, are commonly found in the southern prairies. The giant concrete turtle, designed by Don Foulds, is located in the centre of Turtleford. It is 12 metres long and almost as tall as a single-storey family bungalow. The village of Turtleford (population 505) lies north of Saskatoon on Highway 3.

Turtle   Turtleford, Saskatchewan   1984

Saskatchewan

Originally the site of a fort erected in 1875, the town of North Battleford lies north-west of Saskatoon, at the junction of highways 40 and 4. The area surrounding this Giant Thing is a Western Development Museum that consists of vernacular prairie buildings that have been brought from sites elsewhere and reassembled in North Battleford. This giant Mountie, in his distinctive red tunic, was erected to mark the centennial of both the formation of the Mounties in 1873 and the foundation of the town in 1875.

Mountie and Horse, North Battleford, Saskatchewan 1983

Saskatchewan

Northwest of Saskatoon and west of North Battleford on Highway 40 is the small town of Cut Knife (population 624). This Giant Thing sits in Tomahawk Park, in the centre of town, adjacent to the town's community centre. The teepee is made of precast concrete, has a diameter of just under 5.5 metres and measures just over 9 metres high. The tomahawk is made of fibreglass and is 16.3 metres long.

The *Tomahawk and Teepee* were erected in 1971 as part of the Saskatchewan wide celebration, Home Coming '71, which marked the centennial of a series of treaties signed with local Indian bands in 1871.

Tomahawk and Teepee, Cut Knife, Saskatchewan 1983

Saskatchewan

The city of Moose Jaw (population 33,941), west of Regina, copies the old Indian name for the site, a creek that supposedly resembled the outline of a moose's jaw bone. This 7.5 metre high, ferro-concrete moose, sculpted by Don Foulds, sits along the side of the Trans Canada Highway.

moose   moose Jaw, Saskatchewan   1984

Saskatchewan

This Giant Thing was designed by sculptor Don Foulds and sits along the Trans Canada Highway, outside Indian Head (population 1,885), east of Regina.

Indian Head   Indian Head, Saskatchewan   1987

Saskatchewan

In 1973 the citizens of Rocanville dedicated this giant 6.5 metre high, bronze coloured Oiler on the edge of town to Ernest Symons for 50 years of active service to the community. Symons, born in 1896, was the founder of Symons Metalworkers Company Limited and the inventor of the Symons Oiler, a trigger-operated squirting oil can which gave a measured squirt of oil through its long, narrow spout.

Oil Can   Rocanville, Saskatchewan   1984

Saskatchewan

This giant steel version of target bow and arrow marks the turn off, along the Trans Canada Highway, to an indoor archery range, just outside of Moosomin (population 2,579) in eastern Saskatchewan. "The *Bow and Arrow* is bigger than it looks in the picture," says Robideau, "and one of the terrific things about it is its simplicity."

Bow and Arrow, Moosomin, Saskatchewan 1987

Manitoba

Boissevain (population 1,660) sits on Highway 10 in southwest Manitoba, just north of the border with North Dakota. The town bills itself as the home of the annual Turtle Derby (which takes place in August) and the Turtle Hall of Fame. This building houses photographs of previous Turtle Derbies and Turtle Derby memorabilia. Behind the giant, 9 metre high turtle is a little fenced-off pool of water in which the annual Turtle Derby champion is placed.

Created by G. Barone, the giant turtle is painted in orange, yellow and green.

Turtle   Boissevain, Manitoba   1984

Manitoba

Dauphin (population 2,943) is on Highway 10 in west-central Manitoba, north of the Mountain National Park. "You'd expect that in Canada beavers would be common Giant Things, but they are not. This is the only beaver that I've found," says Robideau. "If we were still in the fur-trading days the beaver would probably be a more popular symbol because it was more a part of commerce, but now people think of it as a nuisance." This giant cartoonlike beaver is especially unusual – Robideau has found that most Giant things in Canada are designed to look realistic.

Beaver, Dauphin, Manitoba 1984

Manitoba

Created by G. Barone, a monumental mason in Winnipeg, this Giant Thing sits at the junction of highways 325 and 6 in central Manitoba. A plaque attached to the base announces that Ashern is the site of the One-box Sharp Tail Hunt, an annual grouse shoot.

G. Barone has also built a giant camel in Glenboro, Manitoba, and the giant white horse in St. Francis Xavier, Manitoba.

Sharp Tail Grouse   Ashern, Manitoba   1984

Manitoba

This Giant Thing sits beside Highway 6, outside of Lundar, between Winnipeg and Ashern. The area is on the pathway of Canada geese migrating south in the winter. A plaque on the base that supports the giant goose announces: "The Giant Canada Goose, symbol of our community, was brought back from near extinction, through the foresight of Mr. W. A. Murphy and Associates." The goose was designed and constructed by Lawrence King and painted by Marlene Hourd. The erection of the goose, in 1976–77, was sponsored by the Lundar Area Development Board.

"Canada geese are definitely the most popular Giant Things, followed by moose," says Robideau. "In the United States it's giant human figures that you see the most."

Canada Goose   Lundar, Manitoba   1984

Manitoba

This three dimensional billboard is in the centre of Winnipeg, just north of the rail-yards. The cows overlook the Economy Auto Sales used-car lot.

Cow Heads   Winnipeg, Manitoba   1984

Manitoba

Gimli (population 1,550) is 85 kilometres north of Winnipeg, on the southwest shore of Lake Winnipeg. In ancient Norse mythology the town's name means "Great Hall of Heaven." In 1874-76 a series of natural disasters in Iceland forced many islanders to leave, and 200 of them settled near present-day Gimli, in an area originally called New Iceland. This giant Viking, located beside Lake Winnipeg, commemorates the Viking ancestors of these Icelanders. It is believed that in medieval times Vikings ventured to the Gimli area by sailing into Hudson Bay and down the Nelson River to Lake Winnipeg.

Viking   Gimli, Manitoba   1984

Manitoba

Selkirk (population 10,037) is located northeast of Winnipeg on the banks of the Red River. Red River carts were constructed entirely in wood, tied together with leather and not surprisingly were notoriously squeaky. With their two large wheels and two shafts attached to either an ox or pony, they were ideally suited to cover a variety of prairie terrain, from mud to marsh to rough roads. The carts were used by the Metis to ferry buffalo meat, from as far north as Fort Edmonton, south along the Red River to markets in St. Paul, Minnesota. Each cart could carry about 300 kilograms of meat, and by 1860 some 600 carts were making the round trip twice annually. Within a couple of decades steamboats, and then the railway, replaced the carts.

This giant cart is a memorial to the men, animals and carts that plied this trade route.

Red River Cart   Selkirk, Manitoba   1984

Ontario

"In Ontario there are far more Giant Things than in any other province but *per capita* Saskatchewan and Manitoba together probably have the most Giant Things," says Robideau. "After the goose and the moose, I think giant muskie fish are the most common Giant Things."

This giant muskie is made out of fibreglass and stands at water's edge along Highway 17 in Kenora, in northwest Ontario. The area is known for its pulp and paper mills and for its fishing.

Huskie The Muskie, Kenora, Ontario   1982

Ontario

When Robideau first photographed this giant Big Foot hitchhiker in 1982 it was located outside of Vermilion Bay, between Kenora and Dryden, beside a chip stand on Highway 17. When he returned to the area five years later, the figure had moved. Now dressed in a giant pair of floral Bermuda shorts, it stands in front of a Texaco gas station, and Big Foot Auto Parts, in Vermilion Bay. The owner of the gas station has placed a speaker inside the figure. "When somebody goes near it, the owner rushes over to a microphone and goes 'WHARRRRR!' It really frightened our dog," says Robideau.

Formerly the site of an early Northwest Company trading post, Vermilion Bay is now now a small resort town (population 1,130) on Eagle and Red Lakes. The town is also the site of a giant Indian Head.

Mutant Hitch Hiker, Vermilion Bay, Ontario   1987

Ontario

Located beside Highway 17, this 5.5 metres high, ferro-cement bull moose stands next door to the visitor information bureau on the eastern side of Dryden (population 6,640). "This is quite a frightening-looking moose. Most of the other moose that I have seen are rather pleasant looking," says Robideau. "This is certainly larger than the moose in Moose Jaw, Saskatchewan, or Cow Bay, Nova Scotia."

Big Max The Moose, Dryden, Ontario   1982

Ontario

Though variations of the sport were played elsewhere in Europe, curling was first codified in Scotland during the late 18th century and brought to North America soon after by Scottish immigrants. The first official curling club in Canada was the Montreal Curling Club, started in 1807. Thirty years later the same club built the first known indoor curling rink in Canada.

Thunder Bay has been the home of a number of provincial and national championship curling teams. The city (population 112,468), on the extreme northwest edge of Lake Superior, was created in 1970 as result of the union of two adjacent towns, Fort William and Port Arthur. Made out of concrete, this giant curling stone, or "rock," stands on the premises of the Thunder Bay Country Club. On the building behind the "rock" is painted a curling rink bull's eye.

Robideau says that there used to be another giant curling stone in Victoria, B.C., but it has now been taken down. Winston Bronnum of New Brunswick, who sculpted Jumbo the Elephant in St. Thomas, Ontario, has also created a curling stone chip stand in his home province.

Curling Stone　　　Thunder Bay, Ontario　　　1984

Ontario

This giant wooden shoe is an addition to William Snel's single storey bungalow outside Thunder Bay on the road to Kakabeka Falls. Of Dutch descent Snel was formerly a tulip farmer. Snel says that he did not like the idea of having a billboard, but he wanted someway of attracting attention to his business, so he built this giant wooden shoe out of plywood. He uses the giant shoe as a shop for selling bulbs, Dutch chocolates, souvenirs and postcards.

Dutch Shoe   near Thunder Bay, Ontario   1982

Ontario

Nipigon (population 2,466) is located at the mouth of the Nipigon River on the northern edge of Lake Superior, and stands at the junction of Highways 17 and 11, between Thunder Bay and Geraldton. This Giant Thing commemorates a 6.5 kilogram trout caught in the area. "There are lots of Giant Things of muskies," says Robideau, "but this is the only giant trout I have found." Made out of sheet metal it is painted pink and green.

Square Tail Trout   Nipigon, Ontario   1982

Ontario

Beardmore (population 588) is on Highway 11, between Thunder Bay and Geraldton. This claims to be "The World's Largest Snowman". In reality it is a chip and ice cream stand, made out of painted plywood. Robideau has found another snowman in Kenaston, Saskatchewan.

Snowman   Beardmore, Ontario   1984

Ontario

About six kilometres outside of Beardmore, on the sandy shores of Lake Nipigon, is a small park that is home to this 5 metre high figure, *Big Bad John*. Made of wood, the figure was sculpted by Ewald Rentz, who runs a barbershop in Beardmore. Rentz does not limit himself to outside figures. In the windows of his shop are small figures he has made and on the walls are his paintings. Rentz goes on walks in the woods and he looks at the trees. "Sometimes I'll see Donald Duck or Mickey Mouse," he says. He takes the pieces of wood back to the shed behind his barbershop. There he stains the wood and completes the transformation of the branch into the shape he originally saw.

Rentz's sculptures are in the collection of the Museum of Civilization and were included in the 1983 travelling exhibition, *From the Heart: Folk Art in Canada*, mounted by what was then called the Museum of Man.

Big Bad John   Lake Nipigon, Ontario   1984

Ontario

Sudbury (population 90,453) is the site of the World's largest nickel mine. This giant, 9 metre wide *Nickel* is a replica of a Canadian coin issued in 1951 and is made appropriately of sheet nickel. It is located on the highway into town with "a great view of the slagheaps," says Robideau.

Sudbury is also the site of a giant Midas Muffler Chipmobile.

nickel   Sudbury, Ontario   1982

Ontario

The town of White River (population 1,087) is situated on Highway 17, north of Sault Ste Marie in northern Ontario.

Attached to the thermometer is a sign that reads: "The coldest spot in Canada, -72 degrees below zero." Unfortunately, this claim appears to be untrue. The 1977 version of *The Guiness Book of Records (Canadian Edition)* cites the lowest temperature recorded in Canada as -83 degrees F/ -63.8 C. This was on February 3, 1947, in Snag, Yukon Territory. The coldest temperature ever registered in Ontario has been -73 degrees F/ -58.3 degrees C, recorded in Iroquois Falls on January 23, 1935.

Thermometer   White River, Ontario   1982

Ontario

Wawa (population 4,700) is located on the eastern side of Lake Superior, north of Sault Ste Marie, on Highway 101. The name of town means "wild goose" in Ojibway and annually thousands of Canada geese gather over Lake Wawa prior to their migration south for the winter. Made out of painted wrought iron, the *Wawa Goose* is 9 metres high, measures 7 metres from the tip of its beak to the end of its tail, has a wingspan of 6 metres and weighs 2 tonnes.

"Everybody I ever meet who has hitchhiked across Canada has told me that they have waited for ever and ever in front of the giant goose in Wawa for a ride," says Robideau. "One person even claimed they'd waited forty-five days to get a lift – this certainly is 'the world's longest wait by a hitchhiker' I've ever heard about!"

Canada Goose   Wawa, Ontario   1982

Ontario

Located south of Detroit and Windsor, the town of Leamington is the southern-most part of Ontario. The surrounding area is flat, rich farm land and Leamington is the site of a number of canning and bottling factories. While in the town, Robideau bought a postcard of the giant tomato which read "Leamington the Tomato Capital of the World." Evidently this claim has since been modified, and Leamington is now billed as the "Tomato Capital of Canada."

This giant, realistically coloured tomato serves as a visitor information centre and is located in the centre of the town.

"I always get these false directions to Big Things. One time I was in Nova Scotia and some local told me about a 10 metre lobster which I spent a day trying unsuccessfully to find," says Robideau. "When I was in Leamington somebody told me that there was a giant ketchup bottle in front of the Heinz Ketchup factory, so I drove over there. I couldn't find anything, so I asked the security guard where the giant ketchup bottle was. He just looked at me and shrugged his shoulders. He must have thought I was crazy. There was no such thing. Somebody had been pulling my leg."

Tomato   Leamington, Ontario   1986

Ontario

This larger-than-life-size concrete sculpture of Jumbo the circus elephant, in the south-west Ontario town of St. Thomas (population 28,165), commemorates the centenary of Jumbo's death at the hands of a Grand Trunk locomotive in 1885.

Jumbo was hit in his rear by an unscheduled train. The impact derailed the locomotive and mortally wounded Jumbo. P.T. Barnum, who owned the circus, concocted his own version of the accident. He said that Jumbo had stepped in front of the oncoming train, thereby sacrificing his life to save the life of Tom Thumb, a small elephant specializing in stunts. This was not the case. Tom Thumb had in fact been behind Jumbo and was the first to be hit by the train.

Jumbo was created in coloured concrete by Winston Bronnum in his Sussex, New Brunswick, studio, Animal Land. Once completed, Jumbo's legs were separated from his body and the parts were transported on an open flatbed truck from New Brunswick to Ontario along Highway 401.

Jumbo was placed not at the spot where he was hit by the train but on a small square on a ridge overlooking Highway 3 and the entrance to the town. The exact siting of Jumbo divided the town. Which way was he to face? After heated debate it was finally decided to have his head face the square. As result visitors entering St. Thomas are now greeted with a rear-end view of the elephant! Some townsfolk say this is insulting; others feel that this is appropriate, because after all, Jumbo was hit in the rear-end by the locomotive.

Jumbo The Elephant, Saint Thomas, Ontario 1986

Ontario

This giant chicken-on-a-spit is the only known surviving Giant Thing in Toronto. The chicken serves as an outdoor logo for the Chick 'n' Deli Tavern and is located in a small shopping mall on the west side of Mount Pleasant Avenue, just south of Eglinton Avenue East. Below the three-dimensional chicken are flickering red and orange neon flames.

Bar B. Q. Chicken, Toronto, Ontario 1982

Ontario

Carleton Place (population 6,000) is situated southwest of Ottawa. In Perth, Ontario, there is another Giant Thing commemorating the giant 22,000 lb. cheese created in 1892 in Lanark County. Both Carleton Place and Perth's claim to have made the biggest cheese in the world is no longer true. The 1988 edition of *The Guiness Book of Records* notes that in January 1964 a 34,591 lb (15,190 kg) cheddar cheese was made by the Wisconsin Cheese Foundation for exhibition at the New York World Fair.

Cheese　　　　Carleton Place, Ontario　　　1986

Quebec

Point-au-Chêne is a small town on the north side of the Ottawa River on Highway 148 between Hull and Montreal.

Robideau reports that similar drive-in *casse-croûte*, with giant boxes of french fries on their roof, are common in Quebec. In Laval, north of Montreal, he found an old building in the shape of the french fry box – the contents had been lost.

Patates Frites   Pointe-au-Chêne, Québec   1986

Quebec

Outside of Rigaud (population 2,270), beside a gas station on the highway between Ottawa and Montreal stands this giant ice cream cone. In the base of the cone is a booth from which ice creams are sold in the summer. Similar giant cones are common in Quebec. Robideau has found another in St Jerome, Quebec, north of Montreal. Giant ice cream cone stands, dating from the late 1920s, were at one time also common in southern California.

Crème Glacée   Rigaud, Québec   1984

Quebec

A downtown Montreal landmark on Dorchester Boulevard (recently renamed Réné
Lévèsque Boulevard), this giant milk bottle is the three-dimensional logo on the roof of
a building housing a milk company, and served at one time as a water tower.

Bouteille de Lait, Montréal, Québec 1986

Quebec

"In Quebec there are a lot of these mechanical robot figures in front of welding shops, garages or radiator repairshops. This one is on the north side of the Montreal Island. At one time it must have been a repair shop of some sort but later it became a variety store," says Robideau. "Normally they are made out of radiators."

This one in Montreal is made out of the uprights for metal shelving painted black. Outside of a Halifax, N.S. transmission repairshop Robideau found a similar, although smaller, giant mechanical figure, welded together from car transmissions.

Personne Mécanique   Montréal, Québec   1987

Quebec

This is one of the many giant orange "Orange Julep" drive-in restaurants in Quebec. "Many of these oranges are quite smooth and look like orange beach balls, but I like this one most of all. It is pitted and more like an orange that you would pick off a tree," says Robideau. "It's a medium-sized one. The one between the Decarie Expressway and the Blue Bonnets Race Track is much bigger. That one must be almost 15 metres high. This one in St. Jean is about the size of a single-storey house."

St.Jean is south of Montreal, on the west shore of the Richelieu River.

Orange   St. Jean, Quebec   1984

Quebec

Les Chapelets Géants, Cap-de-Madelaine, Québec.

Cap-de-la-Madelaine (population 32,626) is situated on Highway 138 just east of Trois Rivières on the north shore of the St. Lawrence River at its junction with the St. Maurice River. In the mid 17th century it was the site of a Jesuit mission and Notre-Dame du Cap, a stone sanctuary, erected in 1714, is still a popular pilgrimage site today. To build the sanctuary stones were brought from the south side of the St. Lawrence River across the ice in winter. The church was almost complete and the ice began to melt. Prayers were offered the Virgin and the river froze, enabling the rest of the stones to be brought across the river and the building completed.

A bridge, symbolizing the ice, crosses a narrow canal that represents the St. Lawrence River. At mid point across the bridge is a statue of the Virgin Mary. In her hands she holds beads from two giant rosaries that extend from opposite ends of the bridge to the middle. By this act the Virgin connects the two sides of the river in the same way as the ice did.

1984

Quebec

This Giant Thing of a golf ball on a tee sits in the parking lot of *Les Dunes* golf club, outside Sorel on the south shore of the St. Lawrence River.

Balle de Golf, Sorel, Québec 1984

Quebec

St. Jean Port Joli is on Highway 132, on the south shore of the St. Lawrence River and east of Quebec City. The town is known for its folk carvers, who in summers past sold their work from roadside booths. "Now these carvers have shops," reports Robideau "and I guess there must be ten million carvings in the town, certainly enough to supply every Canadian family with at least two each."

These giant carved wooden quill-pens and open books form an entry arch to a camp ground just outside the town.

Plumes et Livres, St Jean Port Joli, Québec 1984

Quebec

"The first time I saw this Giant Thing was at night, and I was coming up from New York City to Montreal by bus, and he was buried up to his knees in snow. A few years later when I was driving in the area I found him again. When I took this photograph in 1984 he was standing beside a *casse-croûte*, and there were also some giant figures of jesters blowing trumpets and a giant ice cream cone on the roof. Since then I have been back again and they all have been taken out. The man is the only thing left. He is now holding a chair, instead of a hot dog and Coke, because the place has become an antique shop."

Homme et Chien Chaud, Sabrevois, Qué. 1984

Quebec

Matane (population 13,900) is on Highway 132 on the eastern end of the Gaspé
Peninsula. Beluga and blue whales are commonly sighted off-shore in the mouth of the
St. Lawrence River. This giant roadside whale souvenir stand is made of sheet metal,
and is painted white with red lips.

Baleine   Matane, Québec   1987

Quebec

The town is located east of Matane, further along on Highway 132, at the tip of the Gaspé Peninsula.

"In this town I saw three or so houses with giant insects and butterflies on their sides, but this house was the best of them all. It had an earthworm, spiders, a centipede and some other big bug," reports Robideau. "This is certainly one of my favourite Big Things, though I must admit I say that about a lot of them!"

Insectes et Araignées, Rivière-au-Renard, Québec 1987

New Brunswick

At exit 344, near the junction of Highways 11 and 134, between Campbellton and Bathurst, stands a garden supply store and this realistically painted, strawberry-shaped building, which is used in summertime as a vending stand for locally grown strawberries.

Fraise/Strawberry, Belledune, Nouveau/New Brunswick 1987

New Brunswick

Giant Log Buildings with Pike Pole and Axe, Boiestown,

Boieston is a logging town on Highway 8, along the Miramichi River in central New Brunswick. These quonset huts, typical of those used in logging camps, are painted to look like split half-logs with a pike pole embedded in one and axe in the other. They form the Woodman's Museum, which shows historical material related to the story of the early settlers and loggers in the area.

ean Brunswick, 1984.

New Brunswick

This giant painted steel magnet marks the site of what is called a "magnetic hill" (which is spelled out in letters across the hill behind the magnet). Nearby is a ferro-cement *Mother Goose* made by Winston Bronnum.

Magnet   Moncton, New Brunswick   1987

New Brunswick

This ferro-cement, 6 metre high potato, with a stylized human face on each side, is the roadside sign for Harvey's Vegetable Stand at exit 312 of the Trans Canada Highway near Fredericton. Robideau believes the potato is a self-portrait of Winston Bronnum, the Sussex, New Brunswick, artist who sculpted it.

Potato Person, Maugerville, New Brunswick 1984

Nova Scotia

In 1979, when Robideau photographed this painted, life-sized wooden carving of
Angus MacAskill, he was located in Halifax. Subsequently he has been moved to St.
Ann's, Cape Breton Island, the town where MacAskill died in 1863.

Billed as the "Cape Breton Giant," Angus MacAskill was born on the Western Isles of
Scotland in 1825. He was reported to have been 236 cm tall, weighed 191.25 kg, had
a shoe size of 14 1/2 and a waist measurement of 203 cm. Known not only for his
great size, but also for his great strength, in the mid 1850s he was part of Barnum's
circus that toured the United States and the Caribbean.

Angus MacAskill   Halifax, Nova Scotia   1979

Nova Scotia

Glooscap is a prominent figure in Eastern Woodland mythology. To sleep at night he is said to have used Nova Scotia for his bed and Prince Edward Island as his pillow. He created many of the geographic features of the area, including the Annapolis Valley and off-shore islands that he threw into the ocean. This giant figure, some 6 metres high, is made of fibreglass and tied to a post in a small downtown park in Parrsboro.

Glooscap   Parrsboro, Nova Scotia   1984

Nova Scotia

This moose is situated on the South Shore of Nova Scotia, just outside of Dartmouth, overlooking the ocean.

Moose and Friends, Cow Bay, Nova Scotia 1987

Nova Scotia

Located on the North Shore of Cape Breton is the town of Cheticamp which claims to have "The World's Biggest Lobster Trap." "I've seen other big lobster traps in the Maritimes that you can walk into but this one is by far the biggest, so maybe it *really* is the world's biggest lobster trap," says Robideau.

Lobster Trap   Cheticamp, Nova Scotia   1984

Prince Edward Island

Killer Ant , Bonshaw , Prince Edwar

Island,   *1984*

Prince Edward Island

≺ Located in a wooded picnic ground behind the Car Life Museum in Bonshaw are a giant squirrel, turtle, kangaroo, and canary, and this 2.4 metre long giant ant.

This giant wooden chair is located outside Sherwood's Furniture Store in Charlottetown. "This chair is almost as big as a single-storey house," claims Robideau.

Rocking Chair, Charlottetown, P.E.I. 1987

Newfoundland

Robideau discovered that like the Yukon and Northwest Territories Newfoundland does not have many Giant Things. Located off the Trans Canada Highway outside of Grand Falls is this giant shaft, commemorating the completion of the Trans Canada Highway. A plaque on the shaft announces that the shaft has been given to Newfoundland by Lester B. Pearson. "This one is really a great Giant Thing," says Robideau. "I think that it's funny that it says it right there on the plaque that the shaft has been given to Newfoundland by Canada!"

Giant Shaft, near Grand Falls, Newfoundland.   1984

Newfoundland

When the Genoese explorer, John Cabot (real name Giovanni Caboto), "discovered" Newfoundland for England in 1497, Portuguese fishermen were already there, fishing the rich waters of the Grand Banks off the south east coast of the island. By the early 16th century a number of small Basque, French and Portuguese fishing settlements were dotted along the southern coast of the island. A Portuguese map, dated 1519, marks the site of present day St. John with the name "Rio de Sa Johem." It is perhaps after this early name for the harbour that St. John's got its name.

This giant statue, located in St. John's, across from Confederation Hall, is the memorial to these early Portguese fishermen of the waters of the land they called Terra Nova.

Portuguese Sailor, St. John's, Newfoundland 1984

Index